The Sun Is My Favorite Star

FRANK ASCH

Voyager Books • Harcourt, Inc.

Orlando   Austin   New York   San Diego   London

For information about permission to reproduce selections from this book,
please write Permissions, Houghton Mifflin Harcourt Publishing Company,
215 Park Avenue South, NY, NY 10003.

www.hmhco.com

First Voyager Books edition 2008

Voyager Books is a trademark of Harcourt, Inc., registered in the
United States of America and/or other jurisdictions.

The Library of Congress has cataloged the hardcover edition as follows:
Asch, Frank.
The sun is my favorite star/by Frank Asch.
p. cm.
Summary: Celebrates a child's love of the sun and the
wondrous ways in which it helps the earth and the life upon it.
1. Sun—Juvenile literature. [1. Sun.] I. Title.
QB521.5.A78 2000
523.7—dc21   98-46383
ISBN 978-0-15-202127-6
ISBN 978-0-15-206397-9 pb

LEO 10 9 8
4500514660

The illustrations in this book were made from black line drawings
and Winsor Newton watercolor swatches painted on Arches 55
medium-grade paper, scanned into a Macintosh G3 computer,
and manipulated with the aid of Adobe Photoshop.
The display type was set in HappyJamas.
The text type was set in Plantin.
Printed in China by LEO
Production supervision by Christine Witnik
Designed by Lydia D'moch

To Liz

The sun is my favorite star.

In the morning, it comes

to my window and wakes me up.

While I have breakfast, it sends the mist away

and dries up the morning dew.

Then it waits for me to come out and play.

The sun is my favorite star.

Gliding through the trees above my head …

it follows me everywhere I go.

Its light is bright and hot.

It peeks through a hole in the fence.

It casts my shadow on the wall.

The sun is my favorite star.

Sometimes it plays hide-and-seek with me.

Sometimes it goes away...

…and brings me back a big bouquet.

The sun is my favorite star.

In the evening, it paints

pretty pictures in the sky for me.

Even in the night, it sends

some light to keep me company.

All stars in the sky are beautiful.

But so far...

the sun is my favorite star!